How to Think like Marcus Aurelius.

The Roman Emperor and Stoic Philosophy.

The happiness of your life depends on the quality of your thoughts.

The Storyteller of Philosophy

How to Think like Marcus Aurelius

Copyright © 2021

All rights reserved.

How to Think like Marcus Aurelius

Summary:

CONTENTS:	vi
Chapter 1	13
Biography • Greatness of mind. Works	13
The Character of the Meditations	26
Talks with himself	34
How to have an efficient brain	36
1. Train to fight the autonomic cycle	39
2. Objectivity	40
3. Remove confusion from the mind	44
Everything you need to know	49
CHAPTER 2	51
Marcus Aurelius' advice for a fuller, happier and more balanced life	51
1. Your happiness depends on your thoughts	53
2. Don't waste your energy criticizing, use it to grow	55
3. Accept what you can control and let go of what you cannot control	58
4. Live the present completely	60

5. Prepare for the worst, in the best way............................62

From whom to take advice and whom to emulate 64

What you can control and what you cannot control...........67

Embrace change 71

Problems and obstacles are the way...................................73

Memento Mori (remember you must die)..........................75

   CHAPTER 3...79

Acceptance of duty and difficulty.......................................79

The soul, the rational and human destiny...........................83

Influence on the political conception of Marcus Aurelius...85

The luck of the thoughts of Marcus Aurelius 94

   CHAPTER 4...98

Marco Aurelio Providence, fate or chance?........................98

Conclusion: 108

How to Think like Marcus Aurelius

CONTENTS:

The timeless wisdom of an ancient Stoic can become a companion for your own spiritual journey.

Stoicism is often portrayed as a cheerless, stiff-upper-lip philosophy of suffering and doom. However, as experienced through the thoughtful and penetrating writings of Roman emperor

Marcus Aurelius (121–180 CE), the Stoic approach to life is surprisingly rich, nuanced, clear-eyed and friendly.

From devotion to family and duty to country, to a near-prophetic view of the natural world that aligns with modern physics, Aurelius' words speak as potently today as they did two millennia ago.

Now you can discover the tenderness, intelligence and honesty of Aurelius' writings with no previous background in philosophy or the classics.

This edition offers insightful and engaging commentary that

explains the historical background of Stoicism, as well as the ways this ancient philosophical system can offer psychological and spiritual insight into your contemporary life. You will be encouraged to explore and challenge Aurelius' ideas of what makes a fulfilling life—and in so doing you may discover new ways of perceiving happiness.

The second century CE, Roman emperor Marcus Aurelius was also a Stoic philosopher, and his Meditations, which he wrote to and for himself, offers readers a unique opportunity to see how an ancient person (indeed an emperor) might try to live a Stoic life, according to which only virtue is good, only vice is bad, and the things which we normally busy ourselves with are all indifferent to our happiness (for our lives are not made good or bad by our having or lacking them). The difficulties Marcus faces putting Stoicism into practice are philosophical as well as practical, and understanding his efforts increases our philosophical appreciation of Stoicism.

How to Think like Marcus Aurelius

How to Think like Marcus Aurelius

How to Think like Marcus Aurelius

Chapter 1

Biography • Greatness of mind. Works

Cesare Marco Aurelio Antonino Augusto (also known as Marco Annio Vero) was born on April 26, 121 d. C in Rome. His family, originally from Betica, was important: his father, in fact, was a consul.

The young Marco received an education from the teacher Frontone, who gave him rhetoric lessons. He was also interested in Stoic philosophy. In 138 d. C. was adopted by the emperor Antoninus Pius, for which it took the name of Marco Aurelio Valerio.

The following year the emperor proclaimed him heir to the imperial throne and Marco took the name of Aurelio Cesare, son of Pius Augustus. In 140 d. C. he has held the consular office for five years. In the same year he married Faustina, the daughter of the emperor, with whom he will have two children.

In the following two years, he obtained two other titles that were indispensable for becoming Roman emperor in the future, the Tribunicia Potestas and the imperium Proconsolare. With the end of the empire of Antoninus Pius, in 161 d. C., became emperor together with his adoptive brother Lucio Vero; for the first time in imperial history Rome has two Caesars, but Mark has greater importance in the management of the Empire.

Under his principality, he pursued a policy that was respectful of the Roman Senate and not of an absolutist type. It guaranteed the Senate to express his opinion on the policy he conducts, to decide on countless state affairs, such as the right to express its opinion in the event of declarations of war by other peoples.

He allowed the men of all the Roman Provinces to access all the important administrative offices of the Roman Empire and also tried to create new routes of a commercial nature, trying to come to terms with China.

Among the measures taken by the emperor in internal politics are mentioned: the creation of the registry with which the families should have registered their children within thirty days of birth, the division of Italy into four districts headed by the juridical , the institution of the figure of the praetor who must keep the protections under control, the control of imperial finances in such a way as to guarantee financial means for the construction of important public works such as the rehabilitation of the road network of the Empire.

The greatness of mind of Marcus Aurelius is known in ancient Rome, as he decided to issue numerous provisions to try to improve the living conditions of the slaves, allowing the natural right to be recognized as regards the inheritance; among the initiatives is that of guaranteeing food funds for children.

Another important decision he made was that aimed at

eliminating the practice of torture both towards the most important men of Rome and towards the free men of the Empire.

He guaranteed other rights in favor of slaves, such as the right of asylum for those who leave a certain place to be able to take refuge for a certain period in another. In foreign policy, the emperor will be engaged for the rest of his life in defending the imperial borders.

The Parthians continued to attack the borders of the Eastern Provinces of the

Roman Empire, so Marcus Aurelius sent Lucius True to the Eastern Provinces, which he had to command and defend. In 166 d. C. Vero, leading the imperial troops, managed to defeat the Parthians, showing his great loyalty to the emperor until the last moment of his life.

Thanks to Lucio Vero the situation in the eastern borders of the Empire returned to normal, thus guaranteeing Marcus Aurelius to draw numerous benefits from the peace with the Parthians.

If in the eastern provinces he

managed to have the situation under control, it became difficult for him to manage the situation on the border with the Danube territorial area, where numerous populations (including the Quadi, the Marcomanni, the Vandals, the Buri, the Iagizi), he carried out also numerous actions and vandal raids against the Roman Empire. The latter aim was to seek new territories in which to settle and, being attracted by the riches of the nearby Roman Empire, they try in every way to undermine it with attacks on the borders.

Furthermore, the situation in this area was difficult for the emperor to manage, since many legions of the Roman Empire at that time left for the Eastern Provinces to fight against the Parthians and because a serious scourge, the plague, began exponentially to wipe out the Roman population, which was halved. These two factors therefore created the weakness of the Danube limes.

Thanks to the help of his brother a few years earlier, he managed to keep the situation under control, since, after the conflict that took place with some North Germanic peoples, peace was reached. After the death of Vero, the populations of the North began to present themselves in a pressing way in the area of Aquileia, north of the Empire and it is difficult for the emperor to manage this great problem.

To put an end to this serious situation, he decided to take matters into his own hands and, being at the helm of the Roman Legions, took part in a series of battles (in the imperial territories of Rezia, Norico, Gallia Cisalpina). Until 175 d.

C. he was forced to settle on the Pannonian front for a long time, as he was involved in various military campaigns against the Germanic populations.

Fortunately, in that year the situation was normalized, but the truce granted by the Germanic populations did not last long; Marcus Aurelius returned to the battlefield and in 179 will lead the Roman army in what will be his last military campaign.

Marco Aurelio Valerio died in Vindobona on 17 March 180 due to the plague. After his principality, the Roman Empire began its inexorable decline also due to the mismanagement of imperial power by Commodus, his son.

"The ambitious man puts his good in the hands of others; the sensual man in the sensations of him; the reasonable man in his actions."

Marco Aurelio.

The Character of the Meditations

"Make yourself free from all other thoughts" - Marcus Aurelius.

"In every instant, in what you are doing, your thoughts are still making yourself your soul free from all other thoughts , only the present moment is what man must feel deprived of". Who is quite predisposed to meditation could write similar sentences?

Except this, the individual in question was not an oriental sage at all, but the well-known Roman emperor of the second century Marcus Aurelius, one of the leading exponents of

Latin Stoicism.

The following passages are taken from the "Talks with himself".

"Who is committing evil is my kinsman, as he participates in a mind and a function that is divine. I cannot be damaged by some defect of others and I cannot be angry with my kindred or even feel my enemy.

We are in the world for mutual help, so any action of mutual contrast is against nature"

(II, 1).

"In every moment, in what

you are doing, let your thoughts be still sure. Make yourself and your soul free from all other thoughts, and you will achieve this only if you attend to each of your works as if it were the end of your existence "

(II, 5).

"If you are not being able to establish what happens in the soul of another, it is not easy for unhappiness to come; on the other hand, great unhappiness necessarily derives from those who do not keep track of the movements of

their own soul "
(II, 8).

"Thinking that it is now possible for you to go out of life", in this way you must complete every work, say your word, and formulate every thought.

"Death and life, fame and obscurity, pain and pleasure, wealth and poverty, all this equally affects the good as well as the bad, as they are neither good nor bad. Therefore, they are neither goods nor evils "
(II, 11).

"Nothing is more miserable than who investigates everything around; and meanwhile he does not realize that only one thing is enough: like pursuing attentively and venerable with enthusiasm the demon that is inside him and only waiting for that. And surely more attentive and venerable he will be able to pursue him if he keeps himself pure from futile vanities; far from criticism, no more he will be discontent with what comes from Gods and men "
(II, 13).

"No one loses a life other than the one he has in that instant; nor does he lives any other life than the one he loses in that instant.

You see well that only the present moment is that of which man must feel deprivation "(II, 14).

"The time of human life is a point; its material substance, a perennial flow; the sensation, darkness; the functions of the organism are a river; those of the soul, dream and vanity; and life is war, a pilgrim's journey; oblivion the voice of posterity.

And now, what can you rely on?

For one thing: Philosophy.

And this thing will allow you to keep the inner demon without violence or harm .

In addition , this demon will have to accept events and everything that happens to him, convinced that everything comes from there, from a mysterious place from which he came one day too. This demon awaits death with serene thought, convinced that it is a simple thing; such as the dissolution of the elements that make up each living being.

Of these elements , each one individually passes without rest from one to the other.

It is a fact that occurs according to nature; and nothing is evil according to nature "

(Book II, 1, 5, 8, 11, 13, 14, 17).

Talks with himself

There is a lot of uncertainty regarding the details of Marcus Aurelius' story, but the clearest picture has been reconstructed through a series of notes he wrote to himself, known as Conversations with himself, or Thoughts and Meditations.

Meditations are one of the most influential works of Stoicism.

It is a timeless manual for learning to live a balanced life.

The "Conversations with himself" also give an idea of the clarity with which Marcus Aurelius thought.

He described the world as it really was rather than as he hoped it would be.

How to have an efficient brain

Every day we are loaded with external stimuli and if we were to absorb each of these stimuli, we would not be able to function properly.

Our brain has efficiency filters, in this way it is able to make a selection of all these external stimuli and allows us to focus on our daily commitments.

He is able to understand what information we need and when. He knows that if you're in a busy restaurant, for example, the sound of the person you're talking to is more important than background noise, so he fits in.

This mechanism, however, unfortunately also has an unwanted side effect.

Michael Kane is a cognitive psychologist from the University of North Carolina who studies the interaction between memory and attention.

In one of his experiments, he sampled a few students of their thoughts at eight random times for one day a week.

Out of 124 participants, he

found that, on average, people were thinking about something completely different than what they were doing about 30 percent of the time.

This demonstrates how easy it is to overlook relevant information and fall into the trap of our brain's default settings.

There are three ways to fight it:

1. Train to fight the autonomic cycle

Through his Meditations, Marcus Aurelius focused on emphasizing the value of looking beyond what we intuitively see on the surface in daily life to better understand the world.

Said in the same words as him:

"Nothing has such a power to broaden the mind as the ability to systematically investigate and truly everything happens before your eyes in life."

Although attention is not automatically paid to all relevant information, we can train our brains to be more proactive.

This is where awareness and clear thinking begin.

2. Objectivity

One of the cornerstones of awareness is objectivity.

It is a kind of neutrality that aims to see the world as it is and not through personal judgments and prejudices. It is not easy to grow.

By design, our senses absorb information about where we are, what we're doing, and how we're feeling.

The world bombard us with stimuli and these stimuli follow a different neural path in each of us.

We mostly go through life understanding the world and influencing our behavior as if we were at the center of reality, and that everything around us matters based on how it fits into our narrative.

The Copernican Principle

states that the Earth does not have a privileged position in the universe. Despite its importance to us, on a larger scale, it is not very important.

The same reasoning applies to people. Despite the intensity with which we feel and perceive, much of what happens in the world in general is not just about us.

There is a bigger image: being able to put aside our personal prejudices will allow us to understand reality for what it is.

It is a crucial distinction.

Throughout his work, one thing that stands out about

Marcus Aurelius is his profound ability to step away and out of his own mind to see the world and himself without any emotional attachment.

He helps explaining the depth of his insights into him. He was able to expand his circle of awareness by attuning himself and aspiring to see things from one pair of eyes with more than one singular perspective. It's a very practical tactic and many of us don't use it enough.

Conceptualize your observations as if you were in someone else's body and try to exploit objectivity through a different set of eyes.

3. Remove confusion from the mind

One of the distinctive aspects of the Meditations is that Marcus Aurelius wrote the work only for himself.

By all accounts it seems to be a very personal diary. There is not much coherence or structure in the way it is presented.

This tells us that his purpose for writing was not necessarily to share his wisdom, but it was likely that he practiced cleaning and organizing his own mind.

Dr. James W. Pennebaker is a pioneer in writing therapy and a professor of psychology at the University of Texas at Austin, United States.

The American Psychological Association has recognized his work on the benefits of recording one's thoughts in a journal as one of the most important research in the field.

In 1994 Pennebaker and his team selected some people who had been unemployed for eight months and divided them into three groups. The first group was asked to write about the dismissal and how they felt about it, the second was asked to write, but about nothing in particular, and the third group was not given writing instructions.

The result? Participants who recorded their layoff experiences were significantly more likely to find new jobs in the aftermath of the study. By writing they were able to formally decline the accumulated stress in their minds and become more aligned with what they were feeling.

It gave them the push they needed to understand where they were and where they needed to go.

With his diary, Marcus Aurelius was able to extract the information that wandered restlessly in his mind and organize it into concrete principles to which he could aspire.

This same effect can also be

reached through meditation, or with nature walks and also thanks to some types of physical exercises.

The human mind is very noisy, but by creating a routine that allows us to clarify it, we can make it less "cleaner".

By building a habit that focuses on ordering our weight sets, we can decline the complexity that comes from living in an increasingly crowded world.

Everything you need to know

Awareness is a state of mind that aims to understand reality as close to truth as possible.

Marcus Aurelius was a political leader who actively aspired to wisdom and who was primarily guided by knowledge. What prompted Aurelius to successfully lead one of the most powerful empires in history was her ability to harness the clarity of his mind.

The purpose of your awareness defines the outer limit of what you can accomplish.

The more you know, the more accurately you can understand your surroundings, the better you will be in organizing your thoughts.

The ability to think clearly / get clarity in your mind is a key benefit and is a skill that can be acquired like any other skill.

It only takes practice.

CHAPTER 2

Marcus Aurelius' advice for a fuller, happier and more balanced life

In a world saturated with stimuli and anxiety in which relationships are increasingly ephemeral, including the relationship with ourselves, Stoicism stands as a redemptive philosophy. This current of thought that emerged in 300 BC and which many consider to be the "first self-help manual in the history of humanity" starts from three key precepts: developing our "I", caring for others and distancing ourselves from material goods.

1. Your happiness depends on your thoughts

"A man's life is what his thoughts about him make it. Your happiness depends on the quality of your thoughts; therefore, act accordingly and be careful not to entertain yourself in notions inadequate for virtue and reasonable nature.

"Remember that everything we hear is an opinion, not a

fact. All we see is a perspective, it is not the truth ; if something external afflicts you, that pain is not due to the event itself, but to the meaning you give it, and you have the power to eliminate it at any time . You have power over your mind, not over events. Realize this and you will find strength. "

Stoic philosophers viewed self-knowledge as a way to achieve happiness. They believed that much of our unhappiness and frustration are self-induced, because we usually do not react to events but to the idea that we have them. It is about learning to separate facts from our expectations and try to look at them from a more useful point of view.

2. Don't waste your energy criticizing, use it to grow

"The inability to see what is going on in another person's mind rarely makes a man unhappy, but those who do not observe the movements of their own mind cannot help but be unhappy . Don't waste the rest of your life making conjectures about others, unless you are looking for a common good. Imagining what they are doing and why, what they are thinking and what they are planning, stuns you and separates you from your inner guidance.

"I have always wondered why if we love ourselves more than others, we value our opinions less than those of others".

These thoughts of Marcus

Aurelius encourage us to focus on our personal development and to stop worrying about what others think. Dedicating time and energy to mulling over the words and attitudes of others is useless. It is more profitable to spend time and energy on improving as a person. Indeed, we must be aware that we can only influence the thoughts, attitudes and behaviors of others through our example. It is no coincidence that Marcus Aurelius said: "Don't waste time discussing what a good man should be. Be one."

3. Accept what you can control and let go of what you cannot control

"It is ridiculous not to try to avoid your own wickedness, which is possible, and instead trying to avoid that of others, which is impossible. You always have the possibility of not having an opinion. You don't have to be nervous or harass your soul for things you can't control. These things don't ask you to judge them. Leave them alone."

One of the most precious teachings of the Stoics is learning to distinguish the difference between what we can control and what is beyond our control, so it is not worth losing your inner peace. Interestingly, by letting go of the need to control, we free ourselves and reach a new state of mental balance that helps us to make all things flow better. After all, in the words of Marcus Aurelius we read: "nowhere can man find a quiet and peaceful place as in the intimacy of his soul ".

4. Live the present completely

"Don't act like you can live 10,000 years. Death is upon you. While you are alive, when it is still possible, improve as a person!! It is not death that man should fear, but never having lived."

This thought of Marcus Aurelius is not pessimistic, on the contrary, it encourages us to be fully aware of our mortality so that we can give the best of ourselves every day. The fact of living continuously looking to the future or with a look to the past takes away the present. For this reason, he considered that we should not fear death, but not having lived, having spent our whole life doing things that do nothing, that do not allow us to connect with our essence or even become obstacles that prevent us from realizing. our dreams.

5. Prepare for the worst, in the best way

"Start each day by saying to yourself: today I will encounter obstacles, ingratitude, insolence, disloyalty, ill will and selfishness."

One of the most important teachings of the Stoics is the importance of controlling our expectations, which are often the basis of our anger or frustration. Marcus Aurelius does not encourage us to develop pessimistic thinking, but not to have unrealistic expectations, so that reality does not hit us hard. He encourages us to prepare for the worst in the best possible way, so that nothing catches us by surprise and we don't feel so overwhelmed or downcast when adversity knocks on our door. It's about foreseeing all the possibilities, even the ones we don't like, and preparing for the final scenario.

From whom to take advice and whom to emulate

The meditations begin with the lessons that Marcus Aurelius has learned from various people in his life: friends, mentors, relatives. In my opinion this is already something to think about. Especially at a time when the role models (gurus, influencers, superstars ...) are increasingly present in our life and increasingly distant.

And at a time when contact with family and one's origins

seem to be losing meaning.

I see myself in some of these dedications and thanks.

From grandfather Vero an amiable and not irascible character.

Not because my grandfather was necessarily like that, but because I recently felt the need to pay homage to him.

And I owe him something.

From my mother the religious sentiment, generosity and refraining not only from doing harm, but also from the mere idea of being able to do it; and, moreover, a simple life far from the habits of the rich.

From a "general" point of view, this dedication is very interesting.

From my tutor, having not become either Green or Blue, or Parmulario or Scutario; enduring fatigue and contenting myself with little; doing everything by myself and not thinking about the facts of others; not to listen to slander.

I think we should all go to school with the instructor mentioned, probably Euphorion, to reflect more and independently.

And avoid cutting situations that would need a scalpel with

the ax.

What you can control and what you cannot control

The basis of Stoic thought, of which Marcus Aurelius is one of the most illustrious exponents, is what is called the dichotomy of control. Epictetus explains it well in Enchiridion (a sort of stoic manual): "Some things are in our power, while others are not. Within our power there are opinion, motivation, desire, aversion and, in a word, whatever you are doing; our body, our property, our reputation, our office and, in a word, everything that is not of our initiative is not in our power ."

Marcus Aurelius reflects a lot on this point and on how paradoxical our lives are, such as about people's opinions.

"Everyone is as good as the things they care about."

I have often been amazed at how each, while loving himself more than anything else, takes less into account the opinion he has of himself than that of others.

Do not be ashamed of being helped, because it is about fulfilling your duty, like a soldier in the assault on the walls. What is it then, if you, limping, could not climb the parapets alone, but it was possible for you to do so with the help of another?

How many, once very famous, have already been consigned to oblivion and how many who celebrated them have also disappeared!

About what engages our

minds, our work and our concerns.

Few things are enough to be happy: to act at the right moment according to reason and justice, with commitment, energy and good disposition, without getting distracted and keeping one's inner demon always intact and pure, as if at every moment one had to give it back; never expect anything and never escape anything, accepting and doing everything in harmony with nature, and having the strength and courage to always say what you think.

Embrace change

Marcus Aurelius teaches us not to fear change and, re-reading with the eyes of those who are faced with the fastest of changes, they make you smile and cheer up his words.

Why should I fear change? What could possibly happen without it? Change is precisely what is most important to universal nature. Could we take a hot bath without the wood turning into fire? Or feed ourselves, without the food being metabolized? And what other useful operations could be accomplished without the change? Don't you see, then, what analogy there is between your change and that of all other things, and how it is necessary for universal nature too ?

Problems and obstacles are the way

Tiring action is the answer. Or, as Ryan Holiday says "Obstacle is the way". In the thought of Marcus Aurelius there is a real condensate to act. Without waiting, without complaining.

"Living is an art that is more

like fighting than dancing, because we must always be ready and steadfast against unexpected blows that come to us."

Memento Mori (remember you must die)

Heraclitus used to say that "one day is the same as every day". By this he meant that every day is the same length but also that a "good" day can mean a "good" life. From this point of view, scarcity could be a good viaticum.

On the other hand, with modern eyes, who ever wants

to think about their own death?

"A stoic."

Do not think with disdain about death, but look upon it with favor; because even death is one of the things that Nature wants.

Look at how precarious and miserable the condition of man is: yesterday embryo, tomorrow mummy or ashes. And therefore this crumb of time that is granted to you live according to nature and separated from life serenely, like the ripe olive that falls blessing the earth that took it upon itself, and giving thanks to the tree that made it mature.

.

It is necessary that you understand once and for all of which cosmos you are a part and of which rector of the cosmos you have been an emanation, and that a time limit is set for you which, if you have not used it for your serenity, will vanish, and you will vanish. you too, and there won't be another chance.

Remember that even if we could live three thousand years and ten times as much, no one loses any life other than the one they are living, nor can they live any other life than the one they are losing. Therefore, the longer life is just as valid as the shorter one, because what matters is the present, and the present is the same for everyone, therefore even what perishes is the same, and what is lost is only an instant, of the all meaningless. In fact, no one can lose the past or the future, for the simple fact that what we do not possess cannot be taken away from us.

Perform every action as if it

were the last in your life.

CHAPTER 3

Acceptance of duty and difficulty

"Marcus Aurelius decided to hire a servant to be escorted to the squares of Rome. The latter had only one task, whispering in his ear as they filled him with praise" You're only a man, you're only a man! "

Faced with the nonsense of the world and its transient realities, the only way left for the test is the turning in on oneself which gives meaning to one's individual existence, applying the Stoic philosophy, and thus to achieve domination over the passions. Marcus Aurelius seems, however, to express a strong pessimism on the fate of man, withdrawing into himself, through a form of melancholy meditation, and to be partially the prey of their life problems. He feels the duty to fulfill the task of time granted by destiny to reign over the Empire with stoic endurance of every difficulty and pain, personal, family or social: In 149 his twins were born, celebrated by a coin with cornucopias crossed underneath. the busts of the two children and the word happiness of the times. However ,they don't survive long. Titus Aurelius Antoninus and Tiberius Elio Aurelio, these are the names found on inscriptions, who died very early, before 152, and was buried in Hadrian's mausoleum. Mark himself wrote: "please:" I must not lose my son! ", but we must pray:" that I would not want to lose! "" He quoted from the Iliad what he calls "the phrase that everyone knows, to remember being a stranger to pain and fear ":" Leaves, some the wind scatters to the ground., so the race of men "   Iliad 6.146

The soul, the rational and human destiny

As in Seneca and Marcus Aurelius, the soul is distinct and separate from the body, but it is therefore composed of the real soul, understood as spirit, pneuma, or vital breath, and the intellect or executive principle, the seat of spiritual activity. Marco also often quotes Epictetus, with references to diairesis understanding the nature of things, being influenced or not influenced by human will and proairesis the division of practical things, in our faculty, or the property "of others", the rational faculties of man, which allow the discernment and understanding of phenomena, rational and irrational, that of fleeing or of which one must adapt, or not, and also refers to philosophers, non-Stoics, such as Socrates, Epicurus, Plato, Democritus, Heraclitus, and of other examples of great men, but also of the transience of glory and uncertainty about the true destiny of the soul of man.

Influence on the political conception of Marcus Aurelius.

Marco had the reputation of being a philosopher-king, already during his lifetime. He is not able to realize all his ideals of him, due to the contrast between his figure as an intellectual and philosopher and the emperor, head of an empire that was based on the strength of the legions, on the violence and the severity of the law. This contrast remains a trace of bitterness in the Memories, for not being able to do more, for not being able to reconcile the life of the philosopher with that of the emperor, and, being a work written for personal purposes and not for propaganda, it is very likely that he experienced this contrast with the discomfort and suffering. He lived much more austere than a Roman noble, and any senator or citizen, rich, trying to show the clemency of a stoic, on every occasion, but he must also approve of acts of violence, such as the Marcomannic war or religious persecution, because to rule men, even by force, it is the duty of a Roman prince, and he cannot refuse, because the Logos of the universe has decided this, and the Stoic is invited to follow this universal will, and he plays the role to him assigned, however, is well aware that he is as fragile and precarious as any man, fleeing any divinization in the person's life. He has often rather tried to cultivate humility, not to get caught up in the enthusiasm of absolute power, not to underline some aspect of himself, warning against becoming another Caesar ", as he writes, sometimes even belittling himself. According to the biographer of Historia Augusta, it seems that Mark showed, at least initially, all his reluctance to assume imperial power, and that he was forced by the Senate to take over the management of the Res publica after Pius' death. " He must have had a real fear of the imperial power of horror imperii, considering his passion for the philosophical life, but he knew that as a stoic, who he was, what he was dealing with and how to do it. Even if torture and the death penalty were in force in Rome, easily applied to slaves and foreigners, the legislation of many "enlightened" emperors that sought to mitigate or reduce the types of crimes punishable with heavy penalties, as in the past he had already done so, Tito. For Marco, in the wake of Seneca and also going beyond what the latter wrote, and the Greek philosophers, men have united in a universal brotherhood, as partakers of the Logos, guided by the dáimon, fragment of the divine that Zeus gave to every man as his defender or help ":" humanitarian "of the Stoics will be one of the foundations of the idea of human rights, many centuries later, as for the Stoa, as for the Platonists, after all there is a law of nature that overrides the law of human nations, just as surprising it is to find in Marcus Aurelius an invitation to tolerance and universal forgiveness, not in the Christian sense, but as fidelity to the so-called humanitas, which he tried to transfer from philosophy to practice , and lex schiavo Epictetus, Marco made his morality, according to which even slaves are not objects, but people who, although subordinate, in the employ of a boss, and "spiritually" always remain free. Therefore, they must es evenings treated, avoiding all cruelty and respecting their dignity. Unlike the Christians, who often did not spend words in favor of the servile class, the philosophical-juridical movement linked to the liberation policy of the Antonines, according to some, had it not been deeply rooted in the Roman economic system, which was based entirely on slavery , would have meant the de facto abolition of the institution of slavery itself within a century. Mark showed great interest, so that each slave was given a chance to recover their freedom, if the master expressed a willingness to give it back. In fact, it is not said that in case of tampering, brought to his attention by a friend Aufidio Vittorino, and cited by later jurists as a decisive precedent, he favored a slave. Consistent with

Stoicism, a philosophy opposed to slavery, it issued a series of norms favorable to the class, servile, extending the laws already promulgated by its predecessors, starting with Trajan, and reaffirming, for example, the concept of the right of asylum for Fugitive slaves could be punished, and murdered in any way by the master, granting their immunity as long as they were in a temple or any statue of the emperor.

The luck of the thoughts of Marcus Aurelius

Conversations with himself are still considered a literary masterpiece and a document of a life dedicated to duty, as well as a work of philosophy that encompasses the maximum of the stoics, and like the previous Manual, the Diatribes of Epictetus, often mentioned in the Memoirs, Seneca's works were a source of inspiration for many people, composing almost a "Gospel of the Gentiles" or "art of living" is universal. The book was among the readings of Frederick the Great, an enlightened monarch in the eighteenth century - coming to be admired by many intellectuals, throughout the time of the Enlightenment -, John Stuart Mill, Matthew Arnold, Goethe, Leopardi, who called them "philosophy on the throne , Arthur Schopenhauer, Emil Cioran, Lev Tolstoy, who had them printed in paperback for the Russian people, Simone Weil, Michel Onfray, Wen

Jiabao, and Bill Clinton. It is not known to what extent, and given that the writings of Mark were popularized after his death. There are scattered references in ancient literature to the popularity of his precepts, and the Emperor Julian was well aware of the Mark's reputation as a philosopher, even if he does not specifically mention the Conversations with himself. itself, although quoted in correspondence Aretas of Caesarea, in the tenth century, and in the Byzantine Suda, it was published in complete form, like the print, in 1558 in Zurich by Wilhelm Holzmann, from a copy of the Manuscript lost. The only other complete copy of the surviving manuscript, the so-called Vaticanus Graecus 1950, is in the Vatican Library, and dates back to the 14th century.

CHAPTER 4

Marco Aurelio Providence, fate or chance?

Marcus Aurelius was a Roman emperor of the second

century AD: the culminating moment (but in some ways also the beginning of the decline) of the empire's history from a political, economic and military point of view.

Like most of the emperors of his dynasty, that of the Antonines, Marcus Aurelius also adhered to the Stoic philosophy, from which he drew strength and inner balance.

In the famous book "To himself", he addresses himself

precisely, remembering the precepts of good living according to the Stoic vision of the world. In this passage the salient points of this vision emerge clearly: withdraw into yourself; do not trust in the success and adulation of others; remember that you are a tiny and fleeting part of a Whole whose will it is impossible and useless to oppose; find your peace in the awareness of your littleness; maintain a rational attitude (that is, do not get carried away by passions) in the face of the vicissitudes of life. All ideas that we find, very similar, in two other Stoic authors of the Roman era: Seneca and Epictetus (And which also have many similarities with the Buddhist concept of enlightenment: the so-called nirvana or nibbana).

The "To himself", a sort of personal diary, was probably written mostly in the emperor's camp tent, in the cold nights of the North, while he was engaged in wars against the barbarian populations of the Quadi and the Marcomanni, the first who managed to keep the enormous war machine of the empire in check, causing a crack in its defense system that would constantly widen over time .

They are looking for a place of retreat, countryside, seashore and mountains; and you are used to longing for such isolation too . But all this belongs to those who do not have the slightest philosophical education, since it is possible, at any time you wish, to withdraw into yourself; because a man cannot retire to a quieter or more undisturbed place than his soul, especially those who have such principles inside that he just needs to look into them to immediately reach full well-being: and by well-being I mean nothing but the right inner order. So indulge in this retreat continuously and renew yourself; and let the principles be brief and elementary which, as soon as you meet them, will be enough to purge you of all nausea and to take your leave without you feeling annoyed by the things you return to. What, in fact, bothers you? The wickedness of men? Given the terms of the problem - namely, that rational beings exist for each other; that tolerance is part of justice; who are wrong without wanting to - and considering how many already, after having harbored enmity, suspicion, hatred, lie pierced, reduced to ashes, stop it at last! Or maybe your annoyance is also due to the fate that, in the universal order, is assigned to you? He returns in thought to the alternative: "Either providence or atoms", and to all the arguments with which it was proved that the cosmos is like a city. Or maybe you will feel touched by the things of the body? Furthermore it comes to think that the mind does not meddle with the gentle or harsh movements of the vital breath, once it has isolated itself and become aware of its power; and then think about everything you have heard about pain and pleasure, and which you have expressed your consent to. Or will it be the worry of a poor reputation to mislead you? Look at the speed of oblivion that invests everything, the abyss of eternity that extends infinite in both directions, the emptiness of fame, the fickleness and recklessness of those who seem to pay praise, and the narrowness of the place where fame is limited. Because the whole earth is a point: and what tiny corner of the earth is this dwelling? And, here, how many and which are the men who will praise you? Remember, then, that you can withdraw to this little field of yours, and above all do not get upset and do not give yourself too much trouble, but be free and look at reality as a man, as a human being, as a citizen, as a mortal being. And among the principles that will have to be most at hand when you fall back on them, there are the following two. The first: things do not touch the soul, but remain immobile on the outside, while the disturbances come only from the opinion that is formed inside. The second: everything you see, in an instant will be transformed and will no longer be; and constantly think about the transformation of how many things you have witnessed in person.

The cosmos has changed , life is an opinion.

Conclusion:

As mentioned above, Marcus' *Meditations* touch on many more topics than the ones addressed here, but we get further in understanding Marcus if we focus on a topic and see how his remarks on that topic are related to his overall project of reminding himself how a Stoic should live. It would be worth working this out for others of his frequent remarks, such as that we are tiny and temporary fragments in the cosmos, that death takes us all in the end, that we ought to live purposively rather than like mechanical toy.